APR 3 0 2014

24 HOUR HISTORY

THE ASSASSINATION OF JOHN F. KENNEDY

NOVEMBER 22, 1963

Terry Collins

Heinemann
LIBRARY

Chicago, Illinois

© 2014 Heinemann Library
an imprint of Capstone Global Library, LLC
Chicago, Illinois

To contact Capstone Global Library please phone 800-
747-4992, or visit our Web site www.capstonepub.com

Edited by Adam Miller, Abby Colich,
    and John-Paul Wilkins
Designed by Steve Mead
Original illustrations © Advocate Art 2014
Illustrated by Yishan Li
Production by Victoria Fitzgerald
Originated by Capstone Global Library Ltd
Printed and bound in the USA

17 16 15 14 13
10 9 8 7 6 5 4 3 2 1

Library of Congress Cataloging-in-Publication Data
Terry Collins
The Assassination of John F. Kennedy : November 22,
1963 / Terry Collins/ Terry Collins.
    pages cm.—(24-Hour History)
    Includes bibliographical references and index.
    ISBN 978-1-4329-9294-1 (hb)—ISBN 978-1-4329-
9300-9 (pb)

    2013935058

Acknowledgments
We would like to thank Darwin Payne for his invaluable
help in the preparation of this book.

CONTENTS

Arrival in Dallas.. 4

Into the City... 8

Aftermath 22

Manhunt 30

Epilogue.. 36

Death of a President 38

Timeline.. 40

Map of President Kennedy's Motorcade..............41

Cast of Characters 42

Glossary 44

Find Out More 46

Index 48

Direct quotations are indicated by a yellow background.

Direct quotations appear on the following pages: 14, 17, 19, 20, 26, 33, 35.

ARRIVAL IN DALLAS

November 22, 1963. Love Field, Dallas, Texas.

Angel,* you are cleared for landing. The rain has stopped, the sun is shining, and the temperature is 63 degrees.

*Angel: United States Secret Service code name for *Air Force One*.

This trip is turning out to be terrific!

Looks like everything in Texas is going to be fine for us.

After that full-page ad criticizing you appeared in the *Dallas Morning News*, I had second thoughts.

Don't worry, Ken. After all...

I hope so, Mr. President.

A RUDE WELCOME

On the morning of November 22, a large advertisement in the *Dallas Morning News* "welcomed" the president. Below the headline was a string of demands from the American Fact-Finding Committee. The ad questioned Kennedy's policies and patriotism. Despite the crowds of thousands, many in Dallas were not happy about the president's visit.

*Lancer: United States Secret Service code name for President Kennedy.

In addition to the Secret Service, over 400 members of law enforcement are on duty for Kennedy's visit.

The president's insistence on greeting crowds face-to-face frequently worries the agents in charge of his protection.

None. Lancer says the weather is too nice to be cooped up. He'll be riding high with no roof or cover.

What can we do? He is the president.

And here I was relieved to have no rain.

And let me guess...no top for the limo today either?

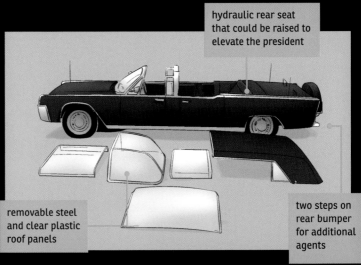

hydraulic rear seat that could be raised to elevate the president

removable steel and clear plastic roof panels

two steps on rear bumper for additional agents

CODE NAME: SS-100-X

Built by the Ford Motor Company and then customized to the specifications of the Secret Service, the presidential limousine began as a 1961 Lincoln Continental convertible. Heavily armored, the car weighed over 7,500 pounds (3,400 kilograms) and was delivered at appearances by a C-130 cargo plane (the same kind of plane used to transport tanks). Custom built, the limousine cost over $200,000.

11:55 A.M.

The presidential motorcade leaves Love Field. President Kennedy is scheduled to speak at 1:00 p.m. at the Dallas Trade Mart.

Vice President Lyndon B. Johnson and his wife, "Lady Bird"

11:56 A.M.

The Texas School Book Depository

Lee, are you coming down? It's about lunchtime.

No, sir. I'm not hungry. I'll eat something later.

Lee Harvey Oswald has worked at the warehouse for five weeks.

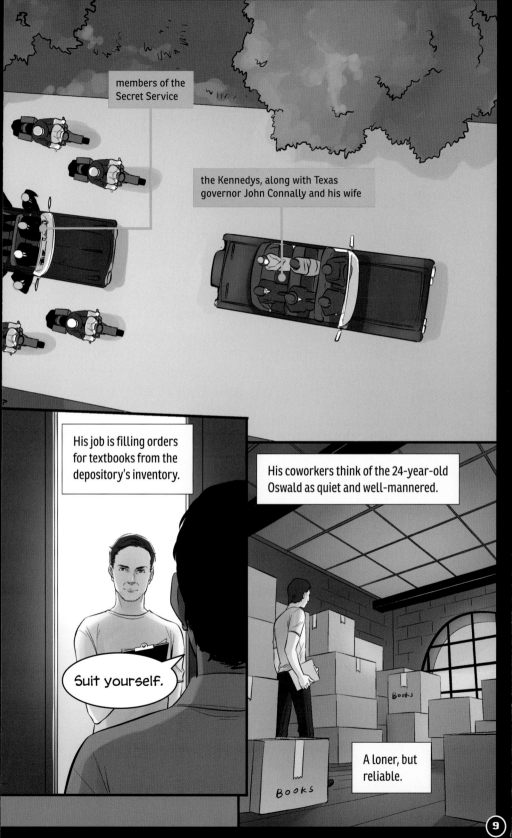

members of the Secret Service

the Kennedys, along with Texas governor John Connally and his wife

His job is filling orders for textbooks from the depository's inventory.

His coworkers think of the 24-year-old Oswald as quiet and well-mannered.

Suit yourself.

A loner, but reliable.

Security becomes very difficult as crowds gather to greet the president.

Progress into the downtown area is slow, but steady.

Hold on, we've got more kids...

...and a nun. A good Catholic has to pay his respects to the sister.

Another stop. Lancer's spotted a nun.

Roger that.

AMERICA'S FIRST CATHOLIC PRESIDENT

The 1960 presidential election was very close. Democrat John F. Kennedy and Republican Richard M. Nixon captivated the American public. Kennedy saw only one major obstacle in his path to victory: his religion. The United States had never elected a Roman Catholic president, and Kennedy feared religious prejudice. However, his religious beliefs proved to be a positive. In the state of New York, the huge Catholic turnout resulted in Kennedy receiving 45 electoral votes. The electoral college ended with 303 votes in Kennedy's column and 219 for Nixon. The popular vote was much closer. Kennedy was elected with 34.2 million votes (49.7 percent) to Nixon's 34.1 million (49.6 percent).

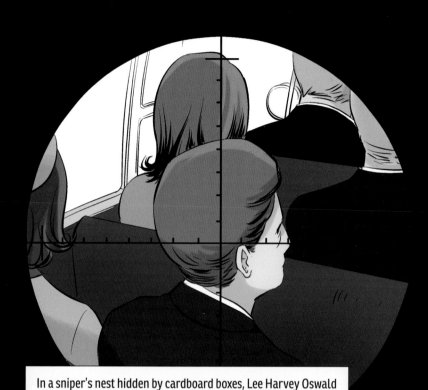

In a sniper's nest hidden by cardboard boxes, Lee Harvey Oswald peers from a window of the book depository and waits.

12:30 P.M.

Looking down at his target, Oswald takes aim and gently squeezes the trigger.

Oswald aims and fires a second time.

BLAM

This shot strikes the president in the throat.

Continuing onward, the bullet travels through the president and strikes Governor Connally.

A third shot cracks downward. In less than 10 seconds, Oswald has fired off three rounds.

The final—and fatal—bullet strikes the president in the head.

AFTERMATH

1:08 P.M.

East 10th Street

Dallas police officer J. D. Tippit, on alert due to the shooting, spots a man hurriedly walking down the sidewalk.

Rumors about the mystery assassin are already spreading. Lacking a good description, the shooter could be anyone.

Still...something about the man's behavior makes Tippit uneasy.

1:22 P.M.

Reports of shots fired reach police investigators, who arrive on the scene of Tippit's murder.

Eyewitnesses point police in the direction Oswald is traveling.

1:36 P.M.

The Texas Theatre, Jefferson Boulevard

Employees at the theater have stepped outside to see the excitement.

CRY OF BATTLE
WAR IS HELL

Using this moment to slip into the movie house, Oswald believes he has gone unnoticed.

Oswald is mistaken. A witness spots him sneaking into the theater and reports this to police.

11:24 A.M.

Two days after Oswald's arrest, in the basement of the Dallas Police Department...

Oswald is being moved to a more secure location, and reporters are on the scene.

Oswald, do you have anything to say in your defense?

Suddenly, a man breaks through the gathered reporters...

Before police can react, he fires a .38 revolver, fatally wounding the alleged presidential assassin.

Oswald's killer is Jack Ruby, a local nightclub owner. Ruby claims his actions saved the Kennedy children from having to return to Dallas for a trial.

With Oswald's death, investigators lose the primary source of information. Many questions about the death of John F. Kennedy will never be answered.

DALLAS
POLICE
36398
11 24 63

DEATH OF A PRESIDENT

On Friday, November 22, 1963, President John F.
Kennedy was assassinated, and a modern-day nation lost
its innocence. Thanks to television and the mass media,
this slaying was uncomfortably real to Americans.
Shot by a sniper while riding in an open convertible
limousine as part of a motorcade through Dealey
Plaza in Dallas, Texas, the president never regained
consciousness. In the automobile along with Kennedy,
Texas governor John Connally was wounded, but was
not the intended target.

Rushed to Parkland Memorial Hospital, the fatally
wounded Kennedy was pronounced dead at 1:00 p.m.
Vice President Lyndon B. Johnson was sworn in as
president at 2:38 p.m. Kennedy's body was flown back
to Washington, D.C., aboard *Air Force One*. An autopsy
was performed at Bethesda Naval Hospital. The fallen
president was buried at Arlington National Cemetery the
following Monday, as the entire country mourned.

On the afternoon of Kennedy's death, Lee Harvey
Oswald, a former U.S. Marine, was arrested at the Texas
Theatre for the crime of shooting Dallas police officer
J. D. Tippit. A former defector to the Soviet Union,
Oswald was later charged with assassinating the
president. Interrogated throughout the weekend,
Oswald insisted he was "a patsy" (scapegoat), and had
not been involved with either shooting.

On Sunday morning, November 24, Oswald was killed on live television in the basement garage of the Dallas Police Station. He was being transferred to a more secure holding location. His murderer was local nightclub owner Jack Ruby. Ruby gave differing accounts of why he shot Oswald, but the primary reason seemed to be revenge for assassinating the president.

On November 29, Lyndon Johnson created a special President's Commission to investigate Kennedy's death. Johnson charged the commission, headed by Supreme Court chief justice Earl Warren, to "evaluate all the facts and circumstances surrounding the assassination and the subsequent killing of the alleged assassin and to report its conclusions and findings…"

With the murder of Oswald, there would be no trial. But the country needed answers. Was there a conspiracy to topple the presidency? Did a foreign nation arrange for Kennedy's death? The Warren Commission gathered evidence from the FBI, the CIA, the Secret Service, and other investigative agencies. Months passed until the commission delivered its findings to President Johnson on September 24, 1964. Their conclusion was that gunman Lee Harvey Oswald had acted alone.

TIMELINE

November 22, 1963

11:40 a.m.	President John F. Kennedy and his entourage arrive in *Air Force One* at Love Field in Dallas, Texas
11:55 a.m.	The presidential motorcade leaves Love Field and makes its way to downtown Dallas, where Kennedy is scheduled to make a speech
12:00–12:28 p.m.	The motorcade follows a route through Dallas, during which the president stops the car several times to talk to citizens
12:30 p.m.	Lee Harvey Oswald shoots President Kennedy. The wounded president is rushed to Parkland Memorial Hospital.
12:31 p.m.	Officer Marrion L. Baker arrives at the Texas School Book Depository, where it is believed the shots were fired from. He asks about Oswald, but allows him to leave after finding out he works at the business.
1:00 p.m.	President Kennedy is pronounced dead at Parkland Memorial Hospital
1:12 p.m.	Lee Harvey Oswald shoots and kills Officer J. D. Tippit
1:22 p.m.	Investigators find a rifle on the sixth floor of the Texas School Book Depository building
1:55 p.m.	Lee Harvey Oswald is arrested at the Texas Theatre
2:04 p.m.	John F. Kennedy's body is taken to Love Field to be carried to Washington, D.C., on board *Air Force One*
2:38 p.m.	Lyndon B. Johnson is sworn in as the 36th President of the United States
11:26 p.m.	Oswald is officially charged with the murder of President Kennedy

The times given in this book are approximate and may vary between sources.

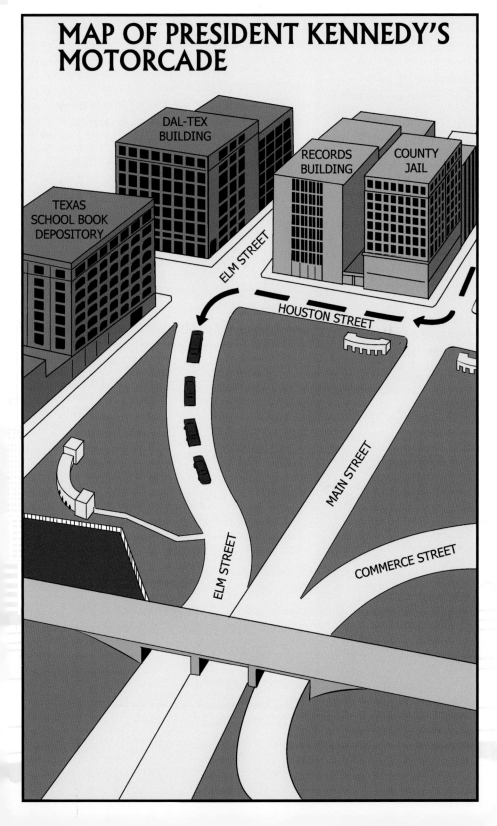

CAST OF CHARACTERS

John F. Kennedy (1917–1963)

The 35th president of the United States was born in Brookline, Massachusetts, on May 29, 1917. At the age of 43, Kennedy was the youngest man ever to be elected president. A war hero and Massachusetts senator before becoming president, Kennedy was also a best-selling author and received the Pulitzer Prize in 1957 for the book *Profiles in Courage*. After winning the election, his time in office from 1961 to 1963 was a time of great promise in the United States. Kennedy was a supporter of the civil rights movement, as well as scientific exploration. He committed the United States to putting a man on the Moon before the end of the decade.

Jacqueline "Jackie" Bouvier Kennedy (1929–1994)

Wife of John F. Kennedy and First Lady of the United States, Jackie Kennedy was noted for being a national trendsetter with her good taste and personal style. Born in Southampton, New York, on July 28, 1929, she was the daughter of wealthy parents who patronized the arts. She married Kennedy on September 12, 1953, and the couple went on to have three children: Caroline, John Jr., and Patrick, who died shortly after birth. After her husband's tragic death, Jackie remarried, and worked as a high-profile book editor for the publishing industry in New York City. She died on May 19, 1994, at the age of 64.

Lee Harvey Oswald (1939–1963)

Born on October 18, 1939, in New Orleans, Louisiana, Oswald was found by the Warren Commission to have acted alone in the assassination of President John F. Kennedy. A high school dropout, Oswald joined the U.S. Marines in 1956 and trained as a sharpshooter. He later moved to the Soviet Union and married Marina Nikolayevna Prusakova. Oswald returned to the United States with his wife and their new child in June 1962. After his arrest for the murders of President Kennedy and Dallas police officer J. D. Tippit, local businessman Jack Ruby murdered Oswald on November 24, 1963.

Jack Ruby (1911–1967)

Born in Chicago, Illinois, on April 25, 1911, Ruby had seven brothers and sisters. Drafted into the U.S. Army Air Forces on May 21, 1943, Ruby never saw combat. In 1947 he moved to Dallas, where he managed several nightclubs and dance palaces. Through his businesses, Ruby was a colorful friend to both felons and policemen alike. On November 24, 1963, Ruby shot and killed Lee Harvey Oswald live on national television. He was convicted of Oswald's murder and sentenced to death, but died in prison on January 3, 1967.

J. D. Tippit (1924–1963)

A Dallas police officer killed by Lee Harvey Oswald on the day of the Kennedy assassination, Tippit was born in Clarksville, Texas, on September 18, 1924. The oldest of six children, the initials *J. D.* were given to him by his father instead of a first name. In 1952 he joined the Dallas Police Department, where he served until the afternoon of November 22, 1963. He was killed instantly after spotting a suspicious-looking man and deciding to question him. That man was Lee Harvey Oswald. Tippit was later given a posthumous Meritorious Citation and Medal of Valor from the Dallas Police Department.

GLOSSARY

autopsy medical examination of a dead body to find the cause of death

boulevard wide city street

Catholic member of the Roman Catholic Church

conspiracy secret agreement among two or more people to do something wrong or illegal

customize make or change according to the specifications of the customer

defector someone who abandons his or her country or cause in favor of an opposing country

depository safe place to keep things

electoral college group of people chosen to help elect the president and vice president of the United States

evidence information that gives reason to believe something

frequently occurring many times; again and again

interrogate question someone at length in a thorough or aggressive way, often for an official purpose

inventory complete list of things in a particular place

motorcade line of vehicles traveling one after another, such as in a parade

patriotism love for and loyalty to one's country

prejudice hatred of a person or group without a just cause or reason

premises piece of property and the buildings on the land

Secret Service branch of the Department of Homeland Security that provides protection for the president

supervisor person who watches over other workers to make sure they are doing a good job

well mannered polite; behaving in a courteous way

FIND OUT MORE

Books

Burgan, Michael D. *John F. Kennedy*. Chicago: Raintree, 2014.

Gormley, Beatrice. *Jacqueline Kennedy Onassis: Friend of the Arts*. (*Childhood of Famous Americans*). New York: Aladdin, 2010.

Sandler, Martin W. *Kennedy Through the Lens: How Photography and Television Revealed and Shaped an Extraordinary Leader*. London: Walker Children's, 2011.

Senker, Cath. *Kennedy and the Cuban Missile Crisis (Days of Decision)*. Chicago: Heinemann, 2014.

DVDs

JFK: 3 Shots That Changed America, History Channel, 2010

The Kennedy Assassination: 24 Hours After, Time Travel Unlimited, 2010

Web Sites

www.archives.gov/research/jfk
The President John F. Kennedy Assassination Records Collection Act of 1992 mandated that all assassination-related material be housed in a single collection in the National Archives and Records Administration (NARA). The resulting collection consists of more than five million pages of assassination-related records, photographs, motion pictures, sound recordings, and artifacts (approximately 2,000 cubic feet of records).

www.csicop.org/si/show/facts_and_fiction_in_the_kennedy
_assassination
An exhaustive overview of the facts and fiction to be found in the wealth of research and published material regarding the Kennedy assassination.

www.jfklibrary.org/JFK.aspx

The life and accomplishments of President and Mrs. Kennedy are covered in extensive and accurate detail here. You can listen to historic speeches, view a media gallery, learn more about the entire Kennedy family, and examine JFK's legacy.

mcadams.posc.mu.edu

A massive depository of research into the assassination, including a focus on debunking the many conspiracy theories that have sprung up regarding the death of the president. A great starting point for beginners or seasoned Kennedy researchers.

Places to Visit

John Fitzgerald Kennedy Birthplace: A National Historic Site

83 Beals Street
Brookline, MA 02446
617-566-7937
www.nps.gov/jofi/index.htm

John F. Kennedy Presidential Library and Museum

Columbia Point
Boston MA 02125
617-514-1600
www.jfklibrary.org

The Sixth Floor Museum at Dealey Plaza

411 Elm Street
Dallas, TX 75202
214-747-6660
www.jfk.org

INDEX

Air Force One 4, 36, 38
American Fact-Finding Committee 5
Arlington National Cemetery 38
arrest 34–35
assassination 16–19
autopsy 38

Baker, Officer Marrion L. 22–23
Bennett, Glen 19
burial 38

Connally, John 9, 17, 18, 38
Connally, Nellie 14
conspiracy 39
crowds, greeting 6, 10, 12

Dallas Morning News 4, 5
death of President Kennedy 33, 38
Democrats 13

Hickey, George 19

injuries 27

Johnson, "Lady Bird" 8
Johnson, Lyndon B. 8, 33, 36, 38, 39

Kennedy, Jacqueline 5, 20, 27, 42
Kennedy, John F. 42
Kennedy, Robert F. 36

limousine 6, 7, 14, 38

motorcade 8–9, 11, 38, 41

news bulletins 26, 33
Nixon, Richard M. 13

oath of office 33, 34
Oswald, Lee Harvey 8–9, 16–17, 18, 20, 24, 30–31, 32, 34–35, 37, 38–39, 43

presidential election 13

Republicans 13
rifle 17, 29
Roman Catholic religion 13
route 41
Ruby, Jack 37, 39, 43

Secret Service 5, 6, 7, 9, 19, 39
Secret Service code names 4, 5
sniper 16, 28, 38

Texas School Book Depository 8–9, 15, 22–24, 28–29
Texas Theatre 32–33, 34
timeline 40
Tippit, Officer J.D. 30–31, 32, 38, 43

Warren Commission 39